BREAKING THE CHAINS OF ADDICTION

BREAKING THE CHAINS OF ADDICTION

AN INTRODUCTION TO ADDICTION-FREE LIFE

Anthony Ordille

Breaking the Chains of Addiction: An Introduction to Addiction-Free Life
Copyright © 2023 by Anthony Ordille. All rights reserved.

Unless otherwise noted, all scripture is from the New King James Version of the Bible © 1982 by Thomas Nelson Inc. Used by permission. All rights reserved.

Scripture quotations taken from the Amplified Bible. Copyright © 1954, 1958, 1962, 1964, 1965, 1987 by The Lockman Foundation. All rights reserved. Used by permission. www.lockman.org.

Inserts about how it works are taken from NA, Narcotics Anonymous Fifth Edition, Copyright © 1982, 1983, 1984, 1986, 1987, 1988 by Narcotics Anonymous World Services Inc. All rights reserved. www.na.org.

Some source of research information outside of endnotes is through the partnership with Foundation for a Drug Free World, © 2006-2022 Foundation for a Drug-Free World. All Rights Reserved. www.drugfreeworld.org.

No part of this publication may be reproduced, stored in a retrieval system, or transmitted by any means, electronic, mechanical, photocopy, recording, or otherwise, without the author's prior permission except as provided by USA copyright law.

Although every effort has been made to ensure that this book's personal and professional advice is valuable and appropriate, the author and publisher do not assume and hereby disclaim any liability to any person, business, or organization choosing to employ the guidance offered in this document.

This book details the author's personal experiences and opinions about addiction and recovery. The author is not a healthcare provider. This information is given to understand that neither the author, publisher, nor any associate of AFL is engaged in rendering legal, medical, or professional advice. In addition, the author, publisher, nor any associate of AFL do not represent or warrant that the information accessible via this book is accurate, complete, or current. Except as specifically stated in this book, neither the author, publisher, nor any associate of AFL, contributors, or other representatives will be liable for damages arising out of or in connection with the use of this book. You understand that this book is not intended as a substitute for consultation with a licensed healthcare practitioner, such as your physician. Before you begin any addiction recovery program or change your lifestyle in any way, you should consult your physician or another licensed healthcare practitioner for any treatment necessary for detoxification or ensure that you are in good health and that the examples contained in this book will not harm you.

www.anthonyordille.com

Cover design by Stas at Getcovers.com
Book Layout © 2017 BookDesignTemplates.com

Addiction-Free Life is located in the United States of America.

ISBN: 9780999627792

1. Self-Help / Substance Abuse & Addictions / General
2. Self-Help / Twelve-Step Programs
3. Religion / Christian Ministry / Counseling & Recovery

Mission

Our vision for addictive behaviors is to see the restoration of the hurt and dying in this world. To help the lost find a place of rest so they can learn how to cope with life in general through love and the help of the Holy Spirit. To be built up in all that our creator has for them.

Our mission is to reach out to the hurting, encourage the weak, and extend hope to the lost. To share the truth about the living word of God and give hope to those struggling with addictions of all kinds. To let them know they can recover through God's Word and live a life of freedom from this crippling disease.

CONTENTS

Chapter One 1
   Types of Addictions 1
Chapter Two 3
   What is Addiction? 3
Chapter Three 13
   Short Story from the Author 13
Chapter Four 15
   Taking the Journey 15
Chapter Five 21
   Recovery vs. Freedom 21
Chapter Six 29
   Myths and Facts 29
Chapter Seven 41
   Living an Addiction-Free Life 41
Chapter Eight 55
   Twelve-Step Comparison 55
Chapter Nine 63
   Vision 63
Suicide Information 67
About the Author 70
Other Books by this Author 72
Connect with Anthony Ordille 73

Chapter One

Types of Addictions

Addictions to Substances
- Alcoholism
- Nicotine (Tobacco)
- Opioids (like heroin)
- Prescription drugs (sedatives, hypnotics, or anxiolytics like sleeping pills and tranquilizers)
- Cocaine
- Cannabis (marijuana)
- Amphetamines (like methamphetamine, known as meth)
- Hallucinogens
- Inhalants
- Phencyclidine (known as PCP or Angel dust)
- Other unspecified substances

Impulse Control Disorders
- Intermittent explosive disorder (compulsive aggressive and assaultive acts)
- Kleptomania (compulsive stealing)
- Pyromania (compulsive setting of fires)

Addictions – Behavioral (Some of these can cross-reference with Impulse Control Disorder)
- Gambling
- Food (eating)

- Sex
- Pornography (attaining, viewing)
- Masturbation
- Using computers / the internet
- Playing video games
- Working
- Exercising
- Spiritual obsession (as opposed to religious devotion)
- Pain (seeking)
- Shopping

    Note: This list is not exhaustive.

Chapter Two

What is Addiction?

It is extremely tough to write on this subject because plenty can be said about addictions of any kind. Whether it is drug use, alcoholism, behavioral or impulse disorder, the road to recovery, what seems to be the right or wrong way to sobriety, and how to stay away from the addiction can be controversial.

There has always been a question from people with addiction problems, "Can I live a life free from addiction?" As with many questions in our society, a wave of different answers opens controversial discussions. On one side of the aisle are those who say, "Once an addict, always an addict." On the other side of the aisle, someone might say, "You never have to live with the addiction again."

I am not sure where you are in this conversation, but I have lived on both sides of the aisle and in between. I understand both parties because I sat in the seat of their discussions. I had to research it myself and then decide wisely from my findings. That is what I am asking from you today. Do not close the door to opportunity just because you may hear something that has rubbed you the wrong way, or go against what you have believed for many years.

Let us jump right in with the definition of addiction:

Source: The Britannica Dictionary[i]
1. *a strong and harmful need to regularly have something (such as a drug) or do something (such as gamble)*
2. *an unusually great interest in something or a need to do or have something*

Source: Merriam-Webster's Dictionary[ii]
1. *the quality or state of being addicted <addiction to reading>*
2. *compulsive need for and use of a habit-forming substance (as heroin, nicotine, or alcohol) characterized by tolerance and by well-defined physiological symptoms upon withdrawal; broadly: persistent compulsive use of a substance known by the user to be harmful*

Addiction is known as a complex disease that can be chronic in nature. Some people do not believe it is a disease but in the person's will. In a way, they are right—at the beginning of one starting out. When someone is addicted to something, it affects the functioning of the brain and body. Therefore, it is a chronic disease of brain reward, motivation, and memory, affecting the network of interconnected neurons in the nervous system, especially the brain. Dysfunction in these areas can lead to characteristic biological, psychological, social, and spiritual manifestations.

This is reflected when there is relief from substance use and other behaviors, so the person will continue the same thing that caused the manifestations in the first place, not because they willed it.

Not only does addiction affect that person, but it also causes severe damage to families and relationships. It can even sometimes affect workplaces and neighborhoods, depending on the type of addiction.

The most common symptoms of addiction are severe loss of control, continued use despite profound consequences, self-absorbent with using, built-up tolerance, and withdrawal.

American Society of Addiction Medicine says:

"Addiction is characterized by the inability to abstain consistently, impairment in behavioral control, craving, diminished recognition of significant problems with one's behaviors and interpersonal relationships, and a dysfunctional emotional response. Like other chronic diseases, addiction often involves cycles of relapse and remission. Addiction is progressive without treatment or engagement in recovery activities and can result in disability or premature death."[iii]

"Addiction is a treatable, chronic medical disease involving complex interactions among brain circuits, genetics, the environment, and an individual's life experiences. People with addiction use substances or engage in behaviors that become compulsive and often continue despite harmful consequences. Prevention and treatment approaches for addiction are generally as successful as those for other chronic diseases."[iv]

The classic hallmarks of addiction include impaired control over substances, behavior, giving full attention to the substance or behavior, continued use despite consequences, and denial, no matter how hard one tries to stop. Habits and patterns associated with addiction are typically characterized by immediate gratification (otherwise known as a short-term reward) coupled with delayed harmful effects, which will lean toward long-term costs.

Physiological dependence occurs when the body must adjust to the substance/behavior by combining the substance/behavior into its "normal" functioning. This state creates the conditions of tolerance and withdrawal. Tolerance is the process by which the body continually adapts to the substance/behavior and requires increasingly more significant amounts to achieve the original effects. This process starts right from the beginning. That is why it is so ludicrous that people say smoking marijuana has no impact on our bodies or that a person willed themselves to the addiction. Withdrawal refers to physical and psychological symptoms people experience when reducing or discontinuing a substance the body has become dependent on. This does not exclude any of the behavioral addictions.

Some of the symptoms of substance withdrawal generally include anxiety, irritability, intense cravings for the substance, nausea, hallucinations, headaches, cold sweats, and tremors, to name a few. The type of impulse control disorder generally includes being violent and having aggressive outbursts, compulsion to steal something that is unnecessary, and lack of control.

Behavioral addiction can lead to gambling cravings, leading to depression, anxiety, insomnia, and physical symptoms. Spending more time alone, less socializing, not trying new experiences, and avoiding conversations lead to an unhealthy life. Other withdrawals are not listed here, so I suggest researching the type of addiction you need to discover more.

As you can see, this term does not just mean a person who is on drugs or alcohol; it can be someone who has an eating disorder, a gambling habit, a lying obsession, or lust —basically, anyone who does things they do not want to do can be symptoms of addiction. You try to will yourself to stop, but you cannot. Maybe it has gotten to the point that you do not even know right from wrong. Life is no longer straightforward.

We saw the meaning of addiction. How about the definition of addict:

Source: The *Webster's Dictionary of the English Language*[v] says it is

1. *a person who is addicted: an addict (v. t.)*
2. *to give (oneself) up to something habitually*
3. *to cause (a person) to depend physiologically on a drug*

Source: The *Merriam-Webster's Collegiate Dictionary*[vi] puts it this way:

1. *to devote or surrender (oneself) to something habitually or obsessively <addicted to gambling*

> 2. *to cause addiction to a substance in (a person or animal)*

Very simply put, addiction is any mind-altering, mood-changing substance or habit that causes a problem in any area of your life.

So far, does this sound like you? Are you struggling with something that you do not want in your life? If you answer yes to these questions, then this book is for you.

How does one know that they have a drug problem, an alcohol problem, a gambling problem, an overeating problem, a lying spirit, or any other addictive behaviors?

- ✓ Ask those people around you is one of the ways
- ✓ Taking an inventory of your life can be remarkably effective way
- ✓ Looking at the people you are spending time together with is a great practice

People with illicit addictions may enjoy the secretive nature of their behavior. They may blame society for its narrow-mindedness, choosing to see themselves as free-willed, independent individuals. Addictions tend to limit people's individuality and freedom as they become more restricted in their behaviors. Imprisonment for engaging in an illegal addiction restricts their freedom within society even more.

Even though the word addict may be used throughout our society, you can reference it to the type of problem you are dealing with. Please note that an addict is anyone who is struggling with an addiction that controls their life; it does not have to be a drug. Addiction is not limited to biochemical substances such as cocaine, alcohol, inhalants, or nicotine. People can experience so-called behavioral addictions. Activities such as gambling, eating, pornography, masturbation, texting, and playing video games are possible to addiction because they provide the opportunity for immediate reward.

Example: The fast reward that occurs in a gambling setting can quickly turn a pastime sport into a compulsive reward, where one cannot voluntarily separate oneself from the activity and can quickly turn into a disruption of funds due to losing substantial amounts of their hard-earned money.

On a smaller scale of the mind-mood control that addiction can cause, how about the frequent cell phone texting many young people do, in which they send and receive hundreds of messages daily? This action contains the conditions for addiction. Many observers contend that it is especially problematic because it can interfere with one of the significant tasks of development-developing effective mechanisms of impulse control.

Addiction can be prevented, treated, and managed with the right attitude and help, and the person must be willing to change.

Here is an article from Psychology Today:[vii]

> *"Addiction is a condition that results when a person ingests a substance (e.g., alcohol, cocaine, nicotine) or engages in an activity (e.g., gambling, sex, shopping) that can be pleasurable but the continued use/act of which becomes compulsive and interferes with ordinary life responsibilities, such as work,*

relationships, or health. Users may not be aware that their behavior is out of control and causing problems for themselves and others.

The word addiction is used in several different ways. One definition describes physical addiction. This is a biological state in which the body adapts to the presence of a drug so that drug no longer has the same effect, otherwise known as a tolerance. Another form of physical addiction is the phenomenon of overreaction by the brain to drugs (or to cues associated with the drugs). An alcoholic walking into a bar, for instance, will feel an extra pull to have a drink because of these cues.

However, most addictive behavior is not related to either physical tolerance or exposure to cues. People compulsively use drugs, gamble, or shop nearly always in reaction to being emotionally stressed, whether or not they have a physical addiction. Since these psychologically based addictions are not based on drug or brain effects, they can account for why people frequently switch addictive actions from one drug to a completely different kind of drug, or even to a non-drug behavior. The focus of the addiction isn't what matters; it's the need to take action under certain kinds of stress. Treating this kind of addiction requires an understanding of how it works psychologically.

When referring to any kind of addiction, it is important to recognize that its cause is not simply a search for pleasure and that addiction has nothing to do with one's morality or strength of character. Experts debate whether addiction is a "disease" or a true mental illness, whether drug dependence and addiction mean the same thing, and many other aspects of addiction. Such debates are not likely to be resolved soon. But the lack of resolution does not preclude effective treatment."

This leaves the question: What are the Causes of Addiction? And why do People have Addictive Behaviors in the first place?

No one has found a specific cause of any addiction besides the use of a substance or activity, and there is still no way to know who will become dependent, no matter how you slice it.

Any substance or activity that can be pleasurable can provide the conditions for addiction. It does not target any one group of people or discriminate on the grounds of education, race, sex, or age.

People take drugs or get caught up in behavioral lifestyles because they want to change something about their lives, eventually becoming the problem.

If you are seeking answers because you are tired of being sick and tired of dealing with addiction, then you are in the right place. Keep reading because Addiction-Free Life is for anyone who wants to get out of the hole that addiction has dug, no matter what kind of addiction it may be.

Now that you learned something about addictions and gained a better understanding of why it is time to walk away from the lifestyle you are currently in, in the following few chapters, I would like to share a little short story about myself, as well as give you a chapter that will show you the difference between recovery versus freedom, followed by a chapter for myths and facts, before sharing with you how to live a life addiction-free.

Hopefully, by the time you get to the Living an Addiction-Free Life chapter, you will be ready to take the step to be free from the addiction, no matter what type of addiction it is. Please move forward with an open mind before making any decisions.

Chapter Three

Short Story from the Author

A short story of my life to understand who I am. If you want to read my full testimony, purchase a copy of my autobiography, An Injection of Faith: One Addict's Journey to Deliverance.

I was born in a Catholic family and went to a Catholic school until sixth grade, when I decided I did not want anything to do with God or religion. I wanted to do my own thing without worrying about him judging me. That is when my life started to go downhill.

One day in school, one of the nuns told me that there was a chalkboard in heaven with my name on it, and there was an angel with a piece of chalk in its hand, and every time I sin, it puts a mark on the chalkboard, and when it is full, I will go to hell. That is when I went home and told my mom I wanted to go to public school because I wanted nothing to do with her religion. I know now what she was trying to do, but that was an ugly thing to tell a young boy.

After that, I ran a lifestyle of drugs, and alcohol, until I was thirty-two years old when I was put in detox for trying to take my own life. That is when I started to read books from Alcoholics Anonymous and Narcotics Anonymous. But there was one problem, they talked about God. The first time I heard someone mention God, I ran out of the meeting with the counselor chasing me, who pulled me into his office and sat me down. He asked why I ran out, with my answer stating that I wanted nothing to do with anything that had something to do with God. He said that since I could not leave if I would do him one favor, every time I came across the word God, I would say, "good orderly direction." I agreed!

The next part of my recovery was for me to go to rehab, where the first part of my recovery journey took place. I could read all the literature with God as my own understanding instead of good orderly direction. I allowed my Heavenly Father back into my life, which was the best decision I could have ever made. That led me to the second part of my journey, which I will share in the next chapter.

Chapter Four

Taking the Journey

I do not know where you are with your addiction or if you are seeking a solution for someone you love, but chances are you need answers to questions. That is what I will try to do; give you some answers to those questions.

As you read in the last chapter, I started in the recovery stages with the traditional twelve-step programs that everyone seems to turn to. It is as if they are the only way to get clean and sober and stay that way. I am not sure why that is, just assuming it is because of the God of your own understanding cliché. Maybe it is because of the acceptance of Court Ordered signatures or because they have been around for a long time, and there are meetings at every corner. Whatever the case, they seem to be helping millions of people around the globe with the lives of addicts being changed. I am in no way knocking them down for what they do. My question is,

"How has their life changed?" "Is there a better way to get clean and sober and stay that way?"

If you enjoy going to meetings day-after-day, week-after-week, month-after-month, and year-after-year for the rest of your life, you are right where you are supposed to be. But, if you are like me and want to go forward without the past dictating who you are or how to live, I found the answer to the question, "Is there more to life than spending my time sitting in a meeting?"

Do you what to see how to have a better life without looking over your shoulder at your past life?

One of the meetings of life is to remember what you were, where you came from, how your past was, good or bad, and move forward. We are not supposed to remember our past by living them out daily. We are to grow from our experiences, hurts, pains, and just about any other emotion we face to move us to be better for ourselves and others.

Here is something that I learned, "you are what you speak." Have you ever heard the saying, "you are whom you hang with?" Well, my point is that when I went to the traditional recovery meetings, I would announce myself as an addict or alcoholic. Maybe even as a recovering addict or recovering alcoholic. I was okay with it at the time because I did not know any better, but each time I did, I was keeping that identity.

Within that time, I returned to the higher power of my youth, and I started learning about who I was. I tried to be good, stay clean, and live right for him, but I did not read the Bible.

Oh, no, he said the "B" word. Is this one of those religious writings? Well, it all depends on how you look at it. Are you okay with going to a meeting or reading one of their books with the word God in it, but you do not want to know him any more profoundly than that? He is the "God of your own understanding," so how you understand it is comfortable. Making something your "Higher Power" to help you stay clean and sober, but not deep enough for you to say it is religious. Then yes, this would be religious to you.

But, if you think of your "Higher Power" as someone with your best interest at heart, you will love the rest of this book.

Let me get back on track. During the nine years, I spent in recovery, I only did what man told me to do, I only spoke the way man told me to say, and I only lived the way man told me I had to live. I felt like a robot, even though my life was tremendously better without the drugs. I was happy until I relapsed and lost everything, even my dignity. My sobriety time went out the door, my wife left, and bankruptcy was to follow. I felt like a real loser and did not know how to turn. I felt like my friends through the program did not have my back.

Lost, Broken, and Ashamed.

At that time, I had a warmth come over me, saying everything was going to be okay. I felt to give my nephew a call who would talk to me about Jesus, the son of God who wants to live in my heart. I rejected his Jesus over the years but understood much of what he was saying because of my youth as a Catholic and even some things that were talked about in the program.

Going against my better judgment, I called him and left a voicemail saying I needed to talk to him. A couple of days later, on October 5, 1998, when he returned my call, I accepted Jesus into my heart, and my life changed beyond anything I could ever imagine. I started to read the Bible, where the real story about true recovery was found. If you do not read the Bible like I did not before all this, you will never see what I saw.

I started to see the world in a new way—hatred turned into love, lying turned into truth, the flowers were brighter, and the sky even looked impressive in the way the clouds would form into shapes, more than I could remember. For the first time in my life, I had a hunger to read the Bible.

I remember a day when all the steps of the twelve-step program came to mind, and I realized that Jesus was the higher power. He put all those steps into one ball and threw it down, and said:

> *It is finished, Anthony; you are no longer an addict. I have removed all desires and have delivered you. You no longer need to proclaim you are a recovering addict. I have washed you as clean as snow, and that is why I died and shed my blood. Rejoice, Anthony, you are a new man, a new creation in Christ.* i.e., 2 Corinthians 5:17, Ephesians 4:24, Colossians 3:10

Of course, I was at a place where I was sick and tired of being sick and tired, flopping around like a fish out of water. So maybe I was more receptive to new things, so I did not have to be in a sea of nothing. Or perhaps it was just what I needed to be a productive member of society.

I chose to believe it was just what I needed, bringing me to the place I was supposed to be all along.

Now I have a new identity!

I am not going further into full disclosure of my life. I only wanted to share some highlights on how I got to where I am at this point, and that way, you understand that I walk the walk, not just talk the talk.

In the following chapter, I will break down the difference between living a life in a recovery setting, and living a life in freedom, otherwise known as deliverance, from addiction.

Chapter Five

Recovery vs. Freedom

It is hard to imagine living an addiction-free life in a world that says addictions are incurable.

The so-called experts have misinformed us for so many years that it has altered how people think about addictions. There is sufficient evidence, both inside the word and outside, to show that God has delivered people with addictions. With the help of the gospel, we are here to show that there is a way to be set free from addiction.

They have claimed that addictions are hereditary; yes, this might be true to a point. They have claimed that once an addict, always an addict—yes, in the world system, this might be true. But in most cases, it is the mind that has changed, as you read in chapter two, and that has people making statements like "I cannot stop…I don't know how to get through this…Every time I try to stop, I end up right back where I was." Whatever the cause, once a person's mind has changed and starts to use or do something differently, like eat or drink too much, that person experiences hopelessness. Yes, the chemical imbalance in the body makes it harder to stop, but that does not make it impossible. Once you become clean—or stop using, or stop doing, or stop eating—for a period, the mind can be changed back to its original form.

Here is a quote from a picture I owned with the caption about focus:

> "Change your thoughts, and you change your world."
> -Norman Vincent Peale

Let us touch base on drugs for a second. Why are so many of them called mind-mood-altering substances? Because they change the mind into a mood that is not the original setting it was made to be. That is why you need to work with scripture to transform it into the mind-mood-altering Word. You will need to change your mind back to "Yes, I can," that is why it is a great idea to take hold of the scripture "I can do all things through Christ who strengthens me" (Philippians 4:13). You have power over all your thoughts if you work at it. You can inherit the same power given to Jesus by the Father, giving you the authority to speak over your situation. You have the power to command the addiction to be gone from you! You have the authority to start to change your mind! You change your mind; you see freedom…or, better said, deliverance from the stinking thinking that controls you.

In twelve-step programs, when they tell you to keep coming back, you return to what you were each time. In a godhead twelve-step program, you stand on where you are going, not where you came from. For the rest of the chapter, I will refer to freedom using the word deliverance. Do not let that word push you too far from what it means, which you will see shortly, but simply put, deliverance is being set free from what was. Scripture puts the claim on what will be, "You have been delivered!" All you need to do is stand with that claim, believe it, and it shall be yours. Proclaim it with your mouth, and it will come to pass, as the Bible says. Jesus took the addiction on the cross for you.

Addiction-Free Life will not work for everybody, even though we believe it could. It will only work for those that honestly believe in the true Higher Power. It will only work for those who genuinely believe God is real and his word means what it says. That is why I wrote "Overcome Addiction by God's Grace: 12-Steps to Freedom," so all who read it will grab ahold of the truth and want freedom from addiction, as I received in 1998.

Again, I would like to mention that when we talk about addictions, we group them together. When we talk about a person who cannot stop going to the casinos, having the same mindset as a person who cannot stop going to the bar, or a person who cannot stop putting a needle in their arm, or a person who cannot stop smoking marijuana, or a person who cannot stop lying, or a person who cannot stop stealing, or a person who cannot stop eating—we are saying that all kinds of substances will lead to the same mindset results. The only difference between them is what it does chemically to the body: Overeating leads to too much sugar. Overgambling leads to too much debt.

Overdrinking causes cirrhosis of the liver. Too many drugs will cause brain damage.

One of the things we like to look at in the difference between recovery and deliverance is that recovery is putting a Band-Aid on an open sore; you may put some ointment on it to help it heal, but the scarring will always be there. Deliverance is having it attended by a physician who will clean the inside, stitch it, seal it, and almost make it new with only a minimum amount of scarring. Though you may look at it and still see an injury. The difference between the two is that one will always be noticeable, and the other could go away.

Here is another analogy we like to consider with the difference between recovery and deliverance: Let us say you are standing on a street corner. It is raining (in some of your situations, it will be a drizzle and, in others, pouring). Recovery would be when someone comes by and hands you an umbrella. It works, but it is not complete. Your legs are still getting soaked, and your feet are still drenched. The deliverance would be when someone comes by and opens the door to their vehicle, and you step in, entirely out from the rain. Complete with a heater to dry you off so that there is no evidence you were even in the rain.

The meaning of *recovery*, according to *Merriam-Webster's Collegiate Dictionary*,[viii] is,

> 1. *the act or process of becoming healthy after an illness or injury*
> 2. *the act or process of recovering*

    3. the act or process of returning to a normal state after a period of difficulty
    4. the process of combating a disorder (such as alcoholism) or a real or perceived problem
    5. the return of something that has been lost, stolen, etcetera

The meaning of d*eliverance*, according to *Webster's Dictionary of the English Language,*[ix] is

    1. liberation from bondage or rescue from danger

In other words, deliverance is getting rid of the junk in your life. It is yours and yours alone and cannot be shared with anyone else. In chapter 5 of Overcome Addiction by God's Grace: 12-Steps to Freedom, the steps are the "Twelve I Haves," not the twelve "we haves." We did not put you in your situation; you did. You may think it was because of your circumstances, but it was your decision, not the circumstances. That is why it is you who has to take the first step. Once you have worked through the twelve steps in chapter 4, you can be assured that God has delivered you. God is the author of life, and you have the authority, which is given by him, to tell the addiction to leave. When our lives reflect the word of God, we will walk in the authority.

One of the most significant differences between recovery and deliverance is that one keeps you in bondage, and the other sets you free. When you are in recovery, you always look over your shoulders to see how you are doing. You are always wondering if you will ever stop thinking about the addiction and for the urge to go away. As the Merriam-Webster Collegiate Dictionary says, it is the process of combating a disorder (such as alcoholism) or any other addictive behavior. When you walk in deliverance according to the word of God, you are free from addiction and no longer need to look over your shoulders. The word will help you renew your mind so that the memory will become less and less as you walk out of this type of recovery.

If we believe that the word of God is accurate and that every word in the Bible has a meaning, then we have to believe that God leans more on deliverance than he does on recovery. In the NKJV Bible, there are only three verses that mention recovery; however, there are ninety-eight verses that talk about deliverance. Remember the word deliverance because the difference between being clean and sober—in other words, abstinence—and proper recovery is in a process called deliverance, something only found in Jesus. Many formulas or phrases are used to present the process, which is available to assist in the recovery process. Still, there is only one way to deliverance, and his name is Jesus.

Deliverance is a one-time act but a lifelong process of being changed and conformed to the image of God. That is why the program Addiction-Free Life (AFL) focuses on deliverance in the sense of letting God remove the addiction from us so that he, and only him, can fill us up with the power and strength to overcome addiction. Once you overcome the addiction, you can fulfill the recovery process according to the webster's dictionary and live a healthier life.

I want to ensure that you understand that just because you get free from the addiction does not mean everything will be perfect in your life. You will still come against adversity and run into a hurdle or two or more. The only difference is that this time when you run into them, you will know where to go for help and, in some cases, learn how to get over them on your own and not turn toward the addiction to cover it up.

In the next chapter, I would like to give you some myths and facts about addiction and living in recovery.

Chapter Six

Myths and Facts

Now, if you made it to this point, you are looking to live a life without the addiction breathing down your neck. That is a fantastic place to be.

Substance abuse is widespread worldwide, but unfortunately, many people do not receive the treatment they need. In the United States alone, in 2018, an estimated 21.2 million people required this treatment. Still, only 3.7 million got it, according to a Substance Abuse and Mental Health Services Administration survey.[x]

Widespread myths about addiction recovery can discourage people from getting help. If you or a loved one is struggling with addiction, do not wait. Get help today, either through the traditional way or God's way; just get help! Here are some myths about addiction recovery that were researched.

Myth: People with addiction need to hit rock bottom.

Fact: Many times, the addict or loved one of the people struggling with an addiction believes that someone must hit rock bottom before they can come out of the addiction. This is a worldly way of thinking, and society has accepted it, and many good people have lost the battle with addiction because of it.

"This has repeatedly been proven to be untrue," says Dr. Omar Manejwala, a psychiatrist and addiction expert. He says there are many things you can do to encourage someone to seek help. "Often, people aren't ready to get help because of stigma or shame," he says. To encourage them to seek treatment, "you can reassure that you aren't judging them."[xi]

Myth: Relapse means treatment has failed.

Fact: After going to treatment and getting sober, some people return to alcohol or drug use. This is known as relapse, and many people think it means treatment has failed. This is a myth, says Paul Brethen, a licensed Marriage and Family Therapist, and Certified Addiction Specialist.

"Recovery is a process, and so is treatment," he says. "It is not uncommon for people to have multiple treatment episodes. Like a medical condition that needs to be treated several times, a person must comply with doctor's orders to see any success."[xii]

The bottom line is, the more a person with addiction applies what they have learned in treatment, the better their chances of recovery.

Myth: Going to a rehabilitation center is the only way to treat addiction.

Fact: "The majority of people who achieve recovery do not go to such programs, although they can be helpful for many," Manejwala says.

Many treatments are available, and people with addiction may try several treatment options before they find the one that works for them. Research has repeatedly shown that there are many paths to recovery.

Myth: Addiction treatment is too expensive.

Fact: Some people believe addiction treatment is expensive and cannot afford addiction recovery. Some treatment options are expensive, but there are plenty of budget-friendly options. If you do your research, you can find help. That is one of the reasons Addiction-Free Life was developed: anyone can get the help they need without tapping the piggy bank, and you only need to purchase a book. Other twelve-step support groups such as Alcoholics Anonymous, Narcotics Anonymous, Celebrate Recovery, and others are helpful, and you only need to buy a book.

Myth: A person with an addiction can easily pick out of the crowd.

Fact: Not every person with an addiction fits the stereotypical picture in your head. Many individuals with a substance use disorder, behavioral issue, or impulse control disorder have jobs and families and look just like you and me.

Myth: Only Substance type drugs are addictive.

Fact: While drugs like cocaine, heroin, and methamphetamines are dangerous and come with many risks, and other types of drugs that are used more recreationally, like alcohol and marijuana, even drugs prescribed by a doctor, like opioid painkillers, addictive behaviors can come in many forms as you saw in the list of addictions in chapter one.

Myth: Rehabilitation does not work.

Fact: Yes, some individuals will indeed relapse after receiving treatment. Addiction is a powerful disease, and it often takes more than one attempt or approach to overcome. But this does not mean that it is not effective. Some people would instead try to fight through their addiction on their own, rather than seek treatment because they believe rehabilitation is a waste of time.

Recovery through treatment is possible. With dedication, addiction treatment can be an effective method of both initial cessation and continued sobriety. The National Institute on Alcohol Abuse and Alcoholism states, "Research shows that about one-third of people who are treated for alcohol problems have no further symptoms one year later. Many others substantially reduce their drinking and report fewer alcohol-related problems."

Myth: People struggling with addiction can stop at any time they want.

Fact: Quitting is not as easy as it sounds. With substance use disorder, there are issues like dependence, where your body physically needs the drug to function. Withdrawal, depending on the drug, can be dangerous.

Myth: If you have an addiction, you do not have enough willpower.

Fact: For years, society has looked at addiction as a failure, that a person is not strong enough to overcome it, or that there is something inherently wrong with them. Today we understand addiction exceptionally differently. Studies have shown that addiction is a disease, not a choice once a person is hooked.

If you are living with any addiction, it does not mean you are weak. It simply means you need help.

There are many avenues to stay clean and sober from addiction, but only one place offers true freedom. That place is in the belief that God himself has, can, and will do it through his word. You can claim him as your Higher Power, but you must trust his word to be that source. I will not force religion down anybody's throat, but I will share what I learned from reading the Bible and the evidence that is found in my testimony.

As I said, I felt lost, broken, and ashamed when I relapsed. I was not sure what was the next road that I was going to take. I knew I did not want to live the way I was any longer. That mindset was the key to the journey that led me to what I am about to share.

I started to read the Bible and was amazed by what I read. I never knew, had seen, or heard anything like it. Here is the scripture that saved my life and turned it into the addiction-free life that I live today:

> *And Jesus went throughout all the cities and villages, teaching in their synagogues and proclaiming the gospel of the kingdom and healing **EVERY** disease and **EVERY** affliction.*
> *Matthew 9:35*

This is only one of the many scriptures found in the Bible discussing healing and being set free from diseases, afflictions, and bondage, like Isaiah 53:4-5, Matthew 8:17, and Psalms 103:3.

When I read that, a light bulb went off in my brain, and I yelled out, "If addiction is a disease, and Jesus healed ALL diseases, then I am healed from the addiction. Not just alcohol, but every addiction I have." I ran to tell my sponsor, and he said, "Oh, Anthony, that stuff does not work that way. I tried to get you to church years ago, but that does not mean you are free from it. You will have to attend meetings for the rest of your life." I said excitedly, "No, Carl, I have been delivered from the addictions." Sadly, I never saw him again after that day, and I have not attended a traditional twelve-step meeting since. Just in case you do not recall, it was October 1998. By the way, one month later, God healed me from smoking, and I have not had a cigarette since, over twenty-three years ago, as this book's writing. Also, he removed my desire for caffeine a few years later.

Do not tell me God is not real!

Because this book is an introduction to living an addiction-free life, I want to share some other myths and facts that I believe stop people from freedom with the rest of this chapter.

Now let us shed some more light on addiction. Whether you are a drug addict or addicted to some other type of addiction, it all works the same. Addiction is not hereditary; in most cases, addiction is a seed planted in one's life by curses, images, and a variety of open doors. You are not an addict hooked on drugs because your ancestors were alcoholics, or maybe Uncle Clyde shot heroin. You may have seen Uncle Clyde high and out of control, or perhaps you saw your mom or dad drunk all the time, stumbling around the house. That is called a seed being planted in one's mind. That was an image that repeatedly played in your subconscious. We have a lot of TV programs, movies, and other media that give us these images that can play havoc in our lives. In a basic sense, it glorifies that image.

You have a problem with addiction because that seed was planted in your life as a curse, either by someone in your past or starting with you as a baby.

Here is an example of a seed being planted without knowing: A baby sitting in a room with mom and dad as they are smoking a joint. The room gets filled with smoke as the baby breathes it in. Now let us advance sixteen years; Mom and Dad wonder why their baby, now sixteen years old, is smoking marijuana (or maybe something worse) even if they have not smoked it for years.

In my life, it was my daughter with the cigarettes who said as a kid that she would never smoke because she did not like the smell. Life happened, pressure set in, and today she smokes. Not because she inherited the addiction, but because of the planted seed.

In both cases, the seed that was planted caused a reaction, a growth.

It is no different than if you took an apple seed and planted it in the ground; you will get an apple tree. You cannot expect to plant an apple seed and get an orange tree. There is only one way to kill that seed, even if it grows into a ripe, fully blossomed, fruit-producing tree. You can stand on the word of God and, with your mouth, curse it right out of your life and then allow it to dry up and wither, never to produce another year, month, week, day, or even a minute of being addicted to the addiction.

To clarify some of the misconceptions that were told to you—that you are an alcoholic, drug addict, gambler, or any other name because it is in your bloodline or you have an eating problem because it is in the DNA of your family—we are here to tell you, that statement is incorrect despite what so many studies have shown. In my opinion, the only time there is a transfer through the DNA is if a pregnant mother is an addict and used during pregnancy, then the baby most likely will be inflicted with the addiction, which can be treated. When treated, the baby will grow up to be a normal child, which does not mean they will be an addict in their later years just because they were born addicted. The physical cravings have been treated, and the young mind has no reason to feel the withdrawal because there is no seed planted in the subconscious.

There is a testimony in "Overcome Addiction by God's Grace: 12-Steps to Freedom" book from a man who struggled with a lie about who he was. When he was sexually abused as a young child, it started a chain reaction of consequences. First was protecting the secret. Next came a pornography addiction. That was followed by living a double life. At age nineteen, the secret was exposed, and with it came freedom. Was he born destined to be addicted to porn? Absolutely not! A seed was planted that was allowed to take root until he got a hold of the truth and cursed it one day. Tim's experience shows how the love of Christ can overcome a situation—and the love of people can help change how one lives their life.[xiii]

As was said before, many would say that addictions are incurable; you may even believe that statement yourself. But hundreds of scriptures in the Bible prove otherwise. It is called "The living word of God" because it is over all things!

The only reason we can think why they would say this is that they do not want to believe and trust in the actual living deity who is more significant than themselves. As you read earlier, the Bible says that Jesus has healed all those who believe.

Here are a few diverse ways that it is said:

> *And Jesus went about all Galilee, teaching in their synagogues, preaching the gospel of the kingdom, and healing all kinds of sickness and all kinds of disease among the people.*
> *(Matthew 4:23)*
>
> *But he was wounded for our transgressions, he was bruised for our iniquities; the chastisement of our peace*

> *was upon him; and with his stripes we are healed. (Isaiah 53:5, ASV)*
>
> *Confess your trespasses to one another, and pray for one another, that you may be healed. The effective, fervent prayer of a righteous man avails much. (James 5:16)*

There are so many other scriptures that confess healing to stand behind the myth that once an addict, always an addict. Obviously, they can only be understood if you have an open mind.

Can you see how much God wants to heal you with these few scriptures? Although you may feel physically or mentally drained, there is hope. When a person does not give up, it allows the Lord to move in their life. Allowing Holy Spirit to come into a person's spirit will rejuvenate one's soul. This starts the healing process both inside and out. When you never give up hope, you allow time to adjust your course and return to the right path that you should be on.

The bottom line to this controversy that addictions are incurable is that there is nothing in this world that is not God's or is not put under his feet. "For, He has put all things under His feet." Unmistakably, the main reason why the world says addictions are incurable is that they do not believe and trust in a Divine creator. But when He says, "all things are put under Him," it is evident that He who put all things under Him is excepted" (1 Corinthians 15:27). If you believe the addiction is under his feet, you will walk in victory; and no one can change that, not even the devil himself.

Ok, that was a mouth full; I hope it made sense to you. Sometimes if we do not have the chance to see the other side of things, we do not know they are there. I know that by now, you may not be open to following the same path I took because you fear knowing God any deeper than a higher power of your own understanding. But if you want to be completely set free from the addiction, you need to look to him closer than that.

If you are fed up with where your life is and the addiction has worn you down, I would like to take you to the next chapter to show you how to live a life free from any addiction.

Chapter Seven

Living an Addiction-Free Life

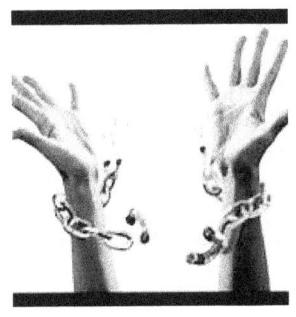

In a world where addiction is made out to be an incurable disease, it is hard to imagine living an addiction-free life. There are programs for every addiction imaginable, but hardly any offer total freedom. They may say it is freedom, but it is not the freedom the Bible discusses. In some cases, people are given the opportunity to get their act together, only to see that the work to stay clean is too hard. The percentage of them getting the help they need starts to decline and lowers every time they try. They give up hope and return to the life they once lived.

It is amazing all the information that can be found on the internet, along with the statistics that will boggle your mind. This is mainly because people are trying to work at getting free from addiction rather than living by faith and letting God remove the addiction.

Some addicts were given a choice to walk away from their addiction but did not know how to cope with life, so they said no. Going away for a few days, weeks, or even months can look promising, but what happens when you need to return to society?

One might ask themselves:

- How am I going to live without getting high
- How can I go out to dinner and not eat all I want
- What happens to the relationships I had; will they forgive me
- How can I face my parents and family knowing I was into porn
- Will I ever find a husband/wife if they know I was a porn star/prostitute
- How can I go to a party and not get drunk
- I love playing cards; will I ever be able to play for fun
- I am in prison; why should it matter

This list can get extremely lengthy on just the questions we have heard. What is your question? You can live life openly and honestly regardless of your question or concern.

You can live in forgiveness, which starts with yourself. Once people begin to see that you have forgiven yourself, they will follow suit. If, for some reason they do not, that is okay too. Just keep forgiving yourself; it is not about what they think but how your Heavenly Father feels about you. Forgiveness is not a gift you give them; forgiveness is a gift you give yourself.

Essentially: living addiction-free means living free.

- No more hidden lies, secrets, deception, stealing, or conning to get what you want
- Exposing everything!

Living free from addiction means working and saving to get what you want.

- Manage your money and time
- Pay your bills and pay them on time
- Watch how you speak
- Being responsible by making your bed and washing your clothes
- Brush your teeth and wash your body
- Watch what you eat and exercise

Number one is to stay healthy: spiritually, physically, and mentally.

A healthy mind means a healthy body. You need to renew your mind, as found in Ephesians 4:22–32. The below scripture reference is a little long, but it shows how powerful scripture is:

> *That you put off, concerning your former conduct, the old man which grows corrupt according to the deceitful lusts, and be renewed in the spirit of your mind, and that you put on the new man which was created according to God, in true righteousness and holiness. Therefore, putting away lying, "Let each one of you speak truth with his neighbor," for we are members of one another. "Be angry, and do not sin": do not let the sun go down on*

> *your wrath, nor give place to the devil. Let him who stole steal no longer, but rather let him labor, working with his hands what is good, that he may have something to give him who has need. Let no corrupt word proceed out of your mouth, but what is good for necessary edification, that it may impart grace to the hearers. And do not grieve the Holy Spirit of God, by whom you were sealed for the day of redemption. Let all bitterness, wrath, anger, clamor, and evil speaking be put away from you, with all malice. And be kind to one another, tenderhearted, forgiving one another, even as God in Christ forgave you.*

This holds true even if you are in an institution. Do not think that just because you are confined within some walls, you do not have to adhere to these principles. You will still have to answer to God for how you live your life once you have been told the truth.

Are you going to finish the race or give up? You will need to know who you are and decide to change your old habits and way of thinking for godly ones.

One suggestion is accountability—finding someone to mentor and help you work the program. You can go to this person if you have any questions or need to discuss your problems. It is also suggested that you make no significant life changes without first discussing it with your accountability partner because bad decisions that lead to failure can be triggers of old behaviors. This is an excellent place to use the buddy system to work the program with. Find someone, or a few people, to share where to get their copy of the program book and work through it together. Refer to the contact information at the back of the book.

The way to overcome the results of a series of bad choices is through a series of right decisions, and sometimes, you will need to do this with someone else. The only way to walk out of trouble is to do the opposite of whatever you did to get into trouble—one choice at a time and not alone. You cannot make a series of bad decisions that result in significant problems and then make one good choice and expect all the results of all those bad choices to go away; that is why you need to seek help. You did not get into deep trouble through one terrible choice; you got into trouble through a series of bad decisions. You cannot do anything about what is behind you, but you can do a great deal about what lies ahead. God is a Redeemer and will always give you another chance to redeem yourself.

On the big picture of recovery God's way, you must build yourself up with hope. A hope that passes all understanding of being a failure and builds on the desire for certain things to happen in your life.

When you have hope, it offers more than addiction. If you walk around all day with the hope of glory in your mind and in your heart, you do not leave enough room for the addiction to take root anymore. Is this easy to do? Of course not. When you live in a world of temptations, you can fall short. That is why you need to pick yourself up and keep company with people who will be there to hold on to you and tell you where you went wrong. Of course, you must be willing to allow them into your world and become transparent with them. If you want them to know you are hurting, you need to tell them what you are struggling with!

In other programs, they will tell you that you must keep going back until the day you die. The author and so many others are proven testimonies that it is just not so. You will, however, keep coming back, not to get a reward from a person but to learn how to seek the Lord and walk in his ways. Just like newborns must depend on their parents to wash and feed them, change their diapers, and rock them to sleep. You will need to be nurtured until you can be weaned off the milk. You will then learn how to feed for yourself and show others to do the same thing. At that point, you will only need to attend meetings for yourself about 1 percent of the time and 99 percent for others. When you give of yourself, there is no time for the addiction to take root. This is how you will grow and earn a medal of honor from your Lord rather than from man.

Freedom from addictions is not hopeless; living in bondage is! You focus on your willingness to walk away from your current lifestyle, learn to be clean, set free from stinking thinking, and fall in love with yourself. You have the desperation to escape from addiction to a new way of living. After you start this, the hope builds until you have a great wall behind you that no devil can get to you. Your future will be wide open for you to walk in, and the skies will be more evident. Just knowing that you are never alone can ease the pain.

If you no longer have the addiction, you will no longer be the person you know now. You will be the person you were born to be. Therefore, if you are struggling with an addiction of any kind or sickness in your body, know that God wants to heal you and set you free, but this can only be done by faith and through his grace. You must see yourself free, clean, and living differently from the lifestyle addiction puts you before it can manifest into the real you.

Faith sometimes works because you believe God's word is alive. As mentioned in the last chapter, one time, the author of this book went on a twenty-eight-day fast for our nation and had no desire to go back to drinking coffee when it was over. Another time before that, he went to a healing service at a church and walked out, not desiring cigarettes. A supernatural power works in every addiction we struggle with, not just the severe cases.

Faith believes in what is true. Two elements can make up faith: First, it is being convinced of the truth and being sure of reality, having evidence of unseen things. The second element is believing, hoping, embracing, and seizing the truth. While faith requires being convinced that what we believe in is true, knowing the truth is only half of faith. To have faith work, you must believe! Do you believe?

Believing is not the same thing as faith. For a belief to be faith, it must illuminate what is undoubtedly true. Belief comes before seeing! Let's use an example of what we mean: Say a friend from the other side of the country flies in to see you. As you are sitting at the table talking, they turn to you and say they came to give you their fully restored Mercedes. You jump up with excitement and ask where it is. They tell you it was being shipped to you and hand you an envelope with the title. You open it up with the thrill that you are now the owner of something you cannot see, but you believe what they said about it being shipped to you is accurate. It is the same basis for believing in God. We cannot see him, yet he has given us a gift for salvation of life. That same intense excitement you would feel for the car should be the same belief in God because the title is the Bible. We can see the writings. We believe that it is attached to what it says it is, just like the title to the car is just a piece of paper—but because of what it says, it makes you the owner.

You may be asking yourself how much faith you need. You only need enough faith to take the first step. If Moses did not take that first step into the water and stuck his staff down into the wet ground, the water would have never parted, and the Israelites would have never been able to cross the Jordan. The Egyptians would have slaughtered them. He trusted God. He heard his voice. God told him to take that path, so he trusted that the voice he heard would get them to the other side. He believed what the Divine Creator told him, and he reacted.

Stop running around the mountain and follow the path of the one who created you, which requires taking a leap of faith. When you take that first step, stay focused on Jesus. When Peter was called out of the boat to walk on the windswept Sea of Galilee toward Jesus, he took his eyes off Jesus and started to sink because fear of drowning came into his mind. The opposite of faith is fear. If you live in fear, you will never experience the potential God has placed in you. Do not let fears of the unknown cripple your destiny because it is your destiny to be free from this addictive behavior.

We can see that scripture gives examples of situations where belief alone is required, even commanded. Just believe! Like Peter walking on water—do not think, just act on what you hear! God requires us to believe in him because he asks us to trust him even when the evidence looks bad. That is why he requires belief and trust in moments of human weakness, but faith is what makes us strong. Faith is the state of being convinced about what we hope for.

It would be best if you had the same faith that is found in the book of Hebrews 11:1:

> "Now faith is the substance of things hoped for, the evidence of things not seen."

Faith is the builder of your future; it opens a decision you must make and stick with. Faith does not come from trying harder; it comes from knowing God. The more you know him because he is faithful, the better your faith becomes, and the more you will trust his word. The way to trust him is to obey him. His path is the most difficult but becomes the most rewarding when you fully surrender to it. Having faith does not mean it is easy or things will come quickly. Having faith is trusting the one who loves you for all the right things at the right time. Sometimes you need to be still, not a passive waiting for something to happen, but a biblical waiting. Apostle Paul says we suffer while waiting for God to set everything right. That means in the waiting time; suffering produces endurance;

endurance produces character, and character produces hope. Hope itself is a form of waiting.

Are you ready to put your faith into action? Are you prepared to believe that what God did for others, he will do for you? Are you willing to believe, even as small as a mustard seed, that the one who created you is whom he says he is? And that he loves you? Addiction-Free Life is here to help you grow your faith, but you must take the first steps.

I hope you heard something from this book and that it has shone a light on your recovery. I had lived in recovery for many years, and now I live in freedom because I saw how God wants me to live free from drugs and not just recover from them. I do not think about how I will stay clean; I rejoice about where I am going without the addiction on my back reminding me who I am. The old man has died, and this new man has been restored to a great life.

Therefore, doing it God's way has more of a guarantee; he has already gone to battle for you, and here is the best part…He won!

Twelve-Step Success Rates

Articles involving Alcoholics Anonymous. Narcotics Anonymous, Cocaine Anonymous, twelve-step group, and twelve-step facilitation in the title or as a keyword were considered for this review.

If you are early in your recovery, perhaps freshly out of a treatment center, the biggest question you probably have is, "What now?" Several outpatient programs and support groups can aid you in your recovery. The most frequently promoted organizations that can assist you in recovery maintenance are, by far, twelve-step programs. Many treatment facilities will either incorporate a twelve-step model into their program or endorse a twelve-step program for aftercare. There is a reason. And it is hard to put it into statistics because success rates can be hard to come by.

Twelve-step support groups' success rates are difficult to identify for several reasons. The most glaring reason that rates and statistics are hard to gauge is that twelve-step organizations' main principle is to remain anonymous. This can make it difficult for a researcher to collect data. Another problem with collecting data is defining what "success" actually means.

Some conclude that success means a lifetime of sobriety. But what about sobriety with instances of relapse? What about individuals who find their life manageable over some time and choose to discontinue a twelve-step program but, in all regards, are successful with sobriety? These examples are hard to classify.

Does it mean the organization failed or succeeded?

There were surveys with a sample group of people, and some studies concluded that twelve-step programs have a minimal margin of success. Other studies show a moderate success rate; others claim a high success rate. In any case, success is best determined by the individual who receives the help rather than by a statistic that is hard to identify. It is indisputable that twelve-step programs do help people, a lot of people. As of 2021, in Alcoholics

Anonymous alone, it is estimated that there are almost two million reported active members.[xiv]

In that same organization that all twelve-step programs are modeled after, I found that they keep a record of their success rates, but in terms of the lengths of sobriety time amongst its active members, not in statistics that show success versus failure. In 2014, the average length of sobriety was eight years. By all accounts, this is indicative of long-term success. Other statistics include:

- Sober less than a year: 27 percent
- Sober for one to five years: 24 percent
- Sober for five to 10 years: 13 percent
- Sober for more than 10 years: 33 percent[xv]

These stats show that it does indeed succeed for some. Another observation that can be made about twelve-step programs, and their success, is that there are over 130 different twelve-step programs that help specific types of addiction. These programs include:

- Narcotics Anonymous
- Overeaters Anonymous
- Gambling Anonymous
- Sex Addicts Anonymous
- Depression Anonymous
- Celebrate Recovery
- Addiction-Free Life

There are twelve-step programs for almost every type of addiction. If the twelve-step model did not work, there would be no reason for varying groups with diverse needs to adhere to the same principles.

Even though there is a need for more public statistics dealing with twelve-step programs, any organization will only be as helpful as the effort you put into it. No program will do everything for you. But what twelve-step programs offer is important: support, acceptance, knowledge, compassion, and a common goal of sobriety. These are the things that will help you in your recovery.

The addiction-Free Life program uses the same twelve-step model as the other programs with education but offers a different lifestyle. It is where you gain the skills you need to combat cravings and get a taste of what your life can look like without addiction using the word of God. Unlike most twelve-step programs, Addiction-Free Life can be used for every known addiction. If you are interested in trying the program, purchase information is found towards the back of the book.

Let's go to the next chapter, where I compare the twelve steps used in most traditional programs and how they relate to the Bible.

Chapter Eight

Twelve-Step Comparison

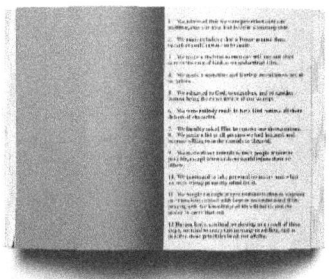

I am not here to bash any twelve-step programs but to show a better way to the truth about who you are and that you can be an overcomer over addictions. The promises of God are real, and they work, so I want to show how the steps used by the traditional programs are taken from the Bible, mostly in part of the content in the meaning of the word of God, then how you can use the word to be delivered from your addictions. The steps are not listed here for copyright purposes, but I referenced Narcotics Anonymous for their twelve steps. xvi

Step 1 says that staying clean must come first. The Bible says in Matthew 6:33 to put God first, and all these things will be added. What things? The help needed is all the truths of the written word coming alive to fulfill scripture. Also, the thing that is necessary for you to overcome the addiction.

Admitting that you are powerless over your addiction and that your life has become unmanageable is a beautiful place to start. But the problem is, no matter what you do to fill the area, it only works briefly. That is why you must keep working on it and keep attending meetings.

That is where I was!

Step 2 is right on, except the power greater than ourselves is the one who made us. Who better to understand the creation than the creator?

Who understands the well-known operating system Microsoft Windows more than anyone else, or who is the one that spent countless hours designing this now worldwide system, Bill Gates, or the people that work in the factories?

Bill Gates, of course!

Those people in the factory learn to understand how it works, but Bill Gates, the mastermind behind windows. That is who our creator is to us, the mastermind of all things (Revelation 1:8). Knowing the end from the beginning, knowing the "ins" and the "outs" of every part of our lives.

Just look at our bodies in how complex they are and how our doctors or scientist are trying to understand them completely, but they cannot! Only the mastermind behind the plan does, and that is why there is no way we evolved from a monkey.

If you are seeking recovery, take this second step and make God your higher power, not the chair you are sitting in or anything else that justifies a higher power.

Step 3 is a good step; it is a powerful step. It is a necessary step but short in one area; we call this salvation (see 1 Thessalonians 5:5–11).

You see, these twelve-step programs are trying to help people from all social classes. The problem is an addiction; no matter what your background or religion you stand on, the god of this world (Satan) does not care what your beliefs are. He is just out to destroy you because God loves you, and he hates him.

There is only one power source that can remove this controlling substance!

Keep reading!

Steps 4 through 9 are a form of deliverance, and it works. You look at getting rid of the garbage in your life to make room for God's love for you. Doing these steps without his help will not be as effective and can leave skeletons in your closet.

Do not do it with shame, guilt, or resentment; be honest about it, and as things are revealed, ask God for forgiveness, and ask him to help you forgive yourself.

Step 5 can be overwhelming, so be careful whom you pick to talk to, and ensure it will be someone other than someone who will draft a story in the local paper. Not everything needs to be said to every person you know. I found out that only those walking in the spirit of God can be trustworthy, and even then, you need to know their walk. God can do magnificent work in this area with you and him in prayer. Prayer is going to the king's throne and letting your petitions be known.

James 5:16 in the amplified Bible says, "To confess to one another, therefore, your faults and pray for one another, that you may be healed and restored to a spiritual tone of mind and heart."

If you back it up a couple of verses, it says, "To call in the church elders and they should pray over him, anointing him with oil in the Lord's name."

See, not just anyone!

Step 6 is a willing step. Are you ready? Remember, when you remove any character defects, you must fill it up with something good, or it will return (see Matthew 12:43–45 and Colossians 3:9–10).

Step 7 is to take action toward a new life step. Believe that the one who made you loves you, and he understands you and wants you to seek after righteousness. He wants you to ask him to clean you so he can fill you with good things. He is the one leading the cheering section.

This is the real reason for the cross! (see Matthew 7:7–12, James 1:5–6, and 1 John 5:14–15).

Step 8 is remarkably close to Habakkuk 2:2, "And the Lord answered me, and said, Write the vision, and make it plain upon tablets, that he may run that reads it."

It is known that if you write it down, you will then see it and understand what you are working with. Now notice that the step says that you became willing to make amends to them all; it does not say to go right out and spill your guts.

God says to make your petition known—him first, and then he will direct our paths to those willing to accept your apology.

This can be a straightforward step if you let it. Refrain from fretting if you cannot do it before your thirty-day medallion. This is a lifetime effort. You do not get here in one day, so you will not be free from forgiveness in thirty days.

First things first, if you ask God into your heart, he is just to forgive you…some of your wrongs…no…all your wrongs. He is the only person you need to worry about forgiving you…besides yourself (see Acts 26:18).

And this leads us to step 9; let God lead you by his Holy Spirit. If you go to someone too early, it can be worse than the wrong you did in the first place. If the person is deceased, write a letter, and go to the grave to bury it or even burn it if you are concerned that someone might see it (see Leviticus 6:4–5).

Step 10 is a form of Luke 9:23–24, daily living in Him and not the drug. When I say the drug, I mean any mind-mood-altering substance!

Step 11 is to be applied to how much you want to leave your old life behind and trust in God for all he has for you without drugs (see Proverbs 3:5–6). Begin having a personal relationship with him and fellowship with other believers (see Ephesians 6:10–18).

That is the importance of the Lord's Prayer in Matthew 6: 9–13. Work in a relationship with him, not working to stay clean. He is faithful and just; all you need to do is ask. He said you have not because you ask not (see Matthew 7:8).

Step 12 is the church assembly (see Acts 14:27, 16:5, 3 John 1:6).

As you can see, God is through the twelve-step programs, even though I did not even touch on the twelve traditions of these programs. There are so many more scriptures that can be used as a comparison. If you read the Bible yourself, you will find them; ask, and he will guide you to them at the appropriate time.

What I hope from the writing of this book is that if you feel you are struggling with getting clean and maybe you have thirty, sixty, ninety, or even two, three, or five years' worth of sobriety medals in your drawer and you want more out of your recovery.

There is a saying you may have heard of. "Work smarter, not harder."

When applying it to your recovery, I would say, "That one day in his courts is better than one thousand days in a traditional twelve-step program (Psalm 84:10)."

This is only part of how much God works in addictions, not just narcotics and alcohol, but all addictions. The name of Jesus is above all names.
(see Ephesians 1:21).

Before you go to the last chapter, I want to share the twelve steps AFL uses.

In chapter five of "Overcome Addiction by God's Grace: 12-Steps to Freedom" book, the steps are the "Twelve I Haves," not the twelve "we haves." We (other people) did not put you in your situation; you did. You may think it was because of your circumstances, but you decided to be in this mess, not the circumstances.

The Twelve "I Haves"

1. I have come to the realization that addiction has ruled my life

2. I have acknowledged that God is the creator and restorer of all things

3. I have decided to confess salvation according to Romans 10:9–10

4. I have made a list of all my sins

5. I have repented with my mouth and asked forgiveness for each one of those sins

6. I have asked God for forgiveness and to remove any guilt or shame I put on myself

7. I have been delivered from all unrighteousness

8. I have asked God to show me all persons I have hurt and made a list

9. I have prayed over my hurt list, seeking those I need to ask forgiveness from

10. I have denied myself and will pick up my cross daily

11. I have made a conscious decision to trust God and live a life of prayer

12. Having had a spiritual experience resulting from these steps, I will try to carry this message to others and uphold these principles in all my affairs, not forsaking a body of believers to fellowship with and call my home.

Chapter Nine

Vision

Provided by 4863882 © Oleg Romanciuk Dreamstime.com

To walk in your newfound life, you must have a vision. In other words, you will need a plan. Everything up to now most likely was not working for you, and your path is leading you to the destruction at hand. Obviously, this is different from where you want to be, or you would not be looking to overcome your past.

You will need to review your objectives and how you will get there. It will be like writing a résumé for a job and selling yourself. You must pursue the heart of God daily to stay focused on the task at hand. You must seek his heart to obtain clarity for your future to stay clear of the addiction. If you do not keep looking forward, you will end up right back where you came from.

Your vision will become more evident with the more time you spend in his presence. Sometimes the cares of this world can cloud your vision, and what appeared to be right was five degrees off the target, and you end up at the wrong place. That is why you must focus on hearing from

God rather than a person because his ways are always straightforward!

Vision is like looking at your life from the Hubble Space Telescope. The Hubble must maintain a steady position in space, and its primary mirror must always remain in proper focus. With this illustration, the primary mirror you need is our creator. If you keep him in line with your vision, he will keep the focus required to reach your destiny. Even though the focus is your responsibility, proper direction requires a consistent yearning for God in every area of your life. Your thoughts must be centered on him, and your passions converge with his. Keep your eye fixed on him; it will be without question when you see the future.

Today you have a choice to make: You can stay where you are and continue to live in your pain, sickness, disease, and the path to destruction, which leads to death. Or you can go through life in a recovery program with the hope that you will never use again. Or you can accept God's way and live your life free of addiction. It is your willingness to know the difference between what is right and what is wrong. God will change your life if you let Him. If you open your heart and mind, he will meet you right where you are.

If you would like to join a twelve-step Christ-centered fellowship that is unlike the traditional twelve-step programs, you can purchase the Overcome Addiction by God's Grace: 12-Steps to Freedom guidebook and workbook to give yourself a chance at a better life.

Overcome Addiction by God's Grace: 12-Steps to Freedom will bring out the best of who you are. It will help you grow in your faith, learn God's word, be an overcomer, and walk over the hurdles in your way. Most importantly, it will help you realize that just because you have made some mistakes, you are not doomed to nonexistence in this society.

AFL's mission is to reach out to the hurting, encourage the weak and extend hope to the lost. To share the truth about the living word of God and give hope to those struggling with addictions of all kinds. To let them know they can recover through deliverance and live a life of freedom from this crippling disease.

Our vision for addictive behaviors is to see the restoration of the hurt and dying in this world. To help the lost find a place of rest so they can learn how to cope with life in general through love and the help of the Holy Spirit. To be built up in all that our creator has for them.

Hopefully, this book has helped answer some, if not all, of your questions. As I said, complete recovery from addictive behaviors can be difficult, but it is not impossible. I live a life free from addiction every day, and most days, I have no concern about addiction or relapse. The only time I think about it is when I am doing research, writing about it, or talking to someone: not because I am trying to stay away from it.

God is no respecter of person; what he did for me, he can do for you. (Acts 10:34)

Because of where I came from and knowing that through many addictions, people sometimes are so tired of the addiction and cannot shake it that they have suicidal thoughts thinking that is the only way they can get away from it. Following this chapter is some information for you if that is where you are.

Suicide Information

Information is taken from the National Institute of Mental Health website.[xvii]

Suicide is a major, and could be a preventable, public health problem. In 2019 Suicide was the tenth leading cause of death in the United States, claiming the lives of over 47,500 people.

The overall rate was 13.9 suicide deaths per 100,000 people. An estimated 11 attempted suicides occur per every suicide death.

Suicidal behavior is complex. Some risk factors vary with age, gender, or ethnic group and may occur in combination or change over time.

What are the risk factors for suicide?

Research shows that risk factors for suicide include:

- depression and other mental disorders, or a substance abuse disorder (often in combination with other mental disorders). More than 90 percent of people who commit suicide have these risk factors.
- prior suicide attempt
- family history of mental disorder or substance abuse
- family history of suicide
- family violence, including physical or sexual abuse
- firearms in the home, in 2019, firearms were the most common method used in

suicide deaths in the United States, accounting for a little over half of all suicide deaths (23,941)
- incarceration
- exposure to the suicidal behavior of others, such as family members, peers, or media figures

However, suicide and suicidal behavior are not normal responses to stress; many people have these risk factors but are not suicidal. Research also shows that the risk for suicide is associated with changes in brain chemicals called neurotransmitters, including serotonin. Decreased serotonin levels have been found in people with depression, impulsive disorders, a history of suicide attempts, and the brains of suicide victims.

If you are in a crisis and need help right away:

Call this toll-free number, available 24 hours a day, every day: 1-800-273-TALK (8255). You will reach the National Suicide Prevention Lifeline, a service available to anyone. You may call for yourself or for someone you care about. All calls are confidential.

*"Thank you for reading,
Breaking the Chains of Addiction: An Introduction to Addiction-Free Life*

Gaining exposure as an independent author relies primarily on word-of-mouth, so if you have the time and inclination, please consider leaving a short-written candid review wherever you can for any books purchased for this author," Amazon, Goodreads, Barnes and Noble, Google, website, etcetera.

It also helps others when considering the book."

Thank you!

Review Links: link.anthonyordille.com/ReviewChannel

If you found this book helpful, please share the title with anyone you know who is struggling with addiction so they can get a copy.

About the Author

Anthony Ordille is the founder of Addiction-Free Life, a Christ-center 12-step recovery program where people are being set free from all kinds of addictions. He lived a life filled with alcohol, drugs, lying, cheating, stealing, adulterous acts, rock-n-roll, basically a destructive lifestyle until he was thirty-two years old when he entered a rehab that introduced him to 12-step programs to help him with recovery. At forty-one, he struggled with alcohol again until he surrendered his life to Jesus Christ in the fall of 1998. Anthony now lives a life free of addictions, and he hopes that through his life experiences, those struggling with addictions will find the truth and follow his lead to a life of hope, peace, and forgiveness.

Anthony became certified as a Therapon Belief Therapist (CBT) at The Therapon Institute Texas. He completed the Associate Degree Program of Christian Studies with a 3.8 (ACS), The Bachelor Degree Program in Church Ministry with a 3.9 (BCh.M), and all his certifications to be a Licensed Minister through The Sure Foundation Fellowship. January 2013 was invited to apply for the Deacon Ministry at Gateway Church, Southlake, Texas. On March 18, 2013, he was ordained in the Deacon Ministry.

Anthony wrote an autobiography, published in 2013. Since then, he has authored books on addiction and developed a Christ-centric Biblical 12-step program. Beyond addiction, Anthony has written several other helpful non-fiction and fiction books for Christian life, including one that would help Christians read the Bible in a year.

He hopes his life experiences will inspire those struggling with addictions to find the truth and follow his lead to hope, peace, and forgiveness through his testimony and the program.

You can connect with Anthony through his website, www.anthonyordille.com, or link.anthonyordille.com/ConnectLandingPage.

Other Books by this Author

Please visit your favorite book retailer to discover other books by Anthony Ordille @ link.anthonyordille.com/Authorcentral or wherever books are sold.

Autobiography
An Injection of Faith: One Addict's Journey to Deliverance

Addiction
Overcome Addiction by God's Grace: 12-Steps to Freedom
Overcome Addiction by God's Grace: 12-Steps to Freedom Workbook
Breaking the Chains of Addiction: An Introduction to Addiction-Free Life
The 5 Essential Ways to Living Addiction-Free—Free Report

Christian Living
My Daily Scriptures: A Day by Day Bible Reading Guide—Here is a book that will help you read the Bible in a year, cover-to-cover, book-by-book.
My Daily Scriptures 365 Day Journal—Companion to guide book or as a standalone journal.

Biblical Fiction Novels
Messiah's Preparation: A Christian Historical Fiction of Jesus in the Wilderness—Previously published as *The Itinerary*.

You may also find the links to these books @ www.anthonyordille.com
If you would like to purchase bulk orders for meetings, please contact AFL through our website.

Connect with Anthony Ordille

Addiction-Free Life is based in the United States of America

Send all inquiries through the website at: www.anthonyordille.com/

I appreciate you reading my book! You can connect with me through my website, www.anthonyordille.com, or link.anthonyordille.com/ConnectLandingPage.

Endnotes

[i] https://www.britannica.com/dictionary/addiction, accessed 5/9/2022.
[ii] *The Merriam-Webster's Dictionary, New Edition*, ©2016 by Merriam-Webster, Incorporated., pp. 9.
[iii] http://www.asam.org/quality-practice/definition-of-addiction, accessed 4/22/16.
[iv] https://www.asam.org/quality-care/definition-of-addiction, accessed 5/9/2022.
[v] *Webster's Dictionary of the English Language*, Based on *The Random House Dictionary*, Classic Edition, copyright © 1983 by Random House, Inc., All rights reserved, pp. 10.
[vi] *Merriam-Webster's Collegiate Dictionary*, "By permission. From *Merriam-Webster's Collegiate® Dictionary*, 11th Edition ©2015 by Merriam-Webster, Inc. (www. Merriam-Webster.com)."
[vii] https://www.psychologytoday.com/basics/addiction, accessed 4/22/16.
[viii] *Merriam-Webster's Collegiate Dictionary*, "By permission. From *Merriam-Webster's Collegiate® Dictionary*, 11th Edition ©2015 by Merriam-Webster, Inc. (www. Merriam-Webster.com)."
[ix] *Webster's Dictionary of the English Language*, Based on *The Random House Dictionary*, Classic Edition, copyright © 1983 by Random House, Inc., All rights reserved, pp. 239.
[x] https://www.samhsa.gov/data/sites/default/files/cbhsq-reports/NSDUHNationalFindingsReport2018/NSDUHNationalFindingsReport2018.htm, accessed 5/11/2022.
[xi] Remark by Manejwala, Omar M.D., Author, Keynote & Addiction Expert, https://www.manejwala.com/.
[xii] Remark by Brethen, Paul, Co-Founder of SoberBuddy, Certified Addiction Specialist, https://yoursoberbuddy.com/.
[xiii] http://www.iamsecond.com/seconds/tim-ross/, Tim Ross's Testimony, iamsecond.com is the website from the I Am Second movement, Dallas-Ft. Worth, Texas, Used by permission from Tim Ross, accessed April 19, 2015.
[xiv] https://www.aa.org/estimated-worldwide-aa-individual-and-group-membership, accessed 5/12/2022

[xv] https://www.aa.org/alcoholics-anonymous-2014-membership-survey, downloaded 5/12/2022
[xvi] Copyright © 1982, 1983, 1984, 1986, 1987, 1988 by Narcotics Anonymous World Services, Inc. All rights reserved. Quote taken from the Fifth Edition, page 17.
[xvii] https://www.nimh.nih.gov/health/statistics/suicide, accessed 5/11/2022.

www.ingramcontent.com/pod-product-compliance
Lightning Source LLC
Chambersburg PA
CBHW050444010526
44118CB00013B/1677